Best wishes for a fine study
and a lovely person,
Aileen Beckman

GIGGLES AND GUFFAWS

GIGGLES AND GUFFAWS

A Handbook of Humorous Books for Children

Aileen K. Beckman

VANTAGE PRESS
New York / Los Angeles / Chicago

FIRST EDITION

All rights reserved, including the right of reproduction in whole or in part in any form.

Copyright © 1989 by Aileen K. Beckman

Published by Vantage Press, Inc.
516 West 34th Street, New York, New York 10001

Manufactured in the United States of America
ISBN: 0-533-08370-2

Library of Congress Catalog Card No.: 88-93124

To Don, Howard, and Brad,
the beloved men in my life,
who never forget how to laugh

Contents

INTRODUCTION	1
PICTURE BOOKS	4
Wordless Picture Books—Preschool to Grade 1	4
Books with Words and Pictures	6
Family Picture Book Humor	12
Realistic Picture Books	22
Eclectic Picture Books	23
FANTASY, TEXTUAL HUMOR—AGES 8–11	26
REALISM—AGES 8 AND UP	32
FANTASY FOR OLDER CHILDREN—8 AND UP	37
PARODY	39
PICTURE BOOKS FOR OLDER CHILDREN—AGES 9–13	44
JOKES, LIMERICKS, AND ZANY POETRY—ALL AGES	47

GIGGLES AND GUFFAWS

Introduction

If you have ever watched children at school or at play, you will know that they laugh a great deal. Their natural exuberance for life is released in free, unrestrained laughter. They laugh at nothing and they laugh at everything: sights, sounds, people, actions, words. They laugh because they are happy and because they love life. It is important to foster and enhance this spirit of fun and there is no more delightful way than sharing humorous books with them. From poetry to prose, and from picture books to textual humor, children and adults can share the scores of delightfully funny books written by outstanding authors. Realistic fiction and fantasy include a wide range of improbable characters engaging in impossible situations designed to produce gales of laughter in children and adults alike. This sharing of laughter and literature can be the place where children are happily introduced to the joy of books. The meeting of literature through laughter can be a natural road to the wider world of literature created especially for children.

This listing includes books published in the United States, Great Britain and Canada which, to the best of my knowledge, are available in the United States in bookstores and libraries.

HOW DOES THE AUTHOR DO IT?

Successful funny texts for children depend upon the funny characters, funny situations, and funny language. The humor is created by somehow manipulating what happens in everyday life. The fat man slips on a banana peel and falls flat on his bottom. This is not how a child pictures an adult, so it becomes funny. This same concept is true in literature. When the ordinary is replaced by the unexpected it becomes humorous. The successful author captures the child's attention by exaggerating details or events, creating eccentric characters or playing with language.

The traditions of fantasy and reality are both present in children's funny books. Fantasy often uses animals as funny characters in order to allow the child a certain feeling of superiority as antics unfold. Besides, animals with human characteristics are much funnier than humans in the same situations. What the author counts on is the sharing of the "fun" of an animal who speaks and acts like a human. Their activities are often commonplace, yet like humans, they get into situations bordering on the catastrophic. Realistic stories use characters and events from a child's world to create a familiar setting for the humor. The author counts on the familiarity of the child's world to help create a natural setting for the humor. Whether fantasy or realism, the author who appeals to the child's sense of humor really understands what makes children laugh.

It is not possible in a handbook such as this to include every humorous book available. There are many. I have endeavored to include a variety ranging from poetry and joke books to contemporary fiction and fantasy. As with any task such as this, the selections are subjective. They made me laugh and they made my students laugh. Read and enjoy! I wish you and your children many hours of laughter.

Picture Books

A true picture book depends upon the equal balance of text and illustrations, both are necessary to create the story. The same is true of humorous picture books. Wise authors and illustrators recognize that young children are captivated by colorful comic illustrations. Characters and situations come alive when the child can actually see them alongside the text. Comic illustrations are generally exaggerated so that the child's sense of humor is tapped even before the text is read. One only has to look at the drawings of Quentin Blake, James Marshall, and Arnold Lobel to see what picturebook humor is all about. The following collection covers a wide range of topics. All are delightfully created to please children and their parents.

WORDLESS PICTURE BOOKS—PRESCHOOL TO GRADE 1

Wordless picture books are a unique humor form. The pictures must be so explicit that the child easily identifies with the author's humor. Only the most talented author/artists succeed and their works lead to exciting storytelling by young children.

CAT ON THE MAT by Brian Wildsmith. New York: Oxford University Press, 1983.

The magic of Brian Wildsmith's picture books is evident in this bright, vivid book in which the words tell one story and the pictures another. The mat, which begins by holding a lone striped cat, becomes increasingly crowded with an assortment of additional animals until an elephant drives the cat to restore tranquility. The humor in the pictures is irresistible.

THE NEST by Brian Wildsmith. New York: Oxford University Press, 1984.

An endearing wordless picture book that tells the story of two birds who build their nest in the branches of a leafless tree. The eggs are deposited and hatch to reveal three dear, little yellow birds. The fun comes to light in the last picture when the branches are revealed in their entirety. The nest is not in a tree at all, but in the antlers of a very accommodating deer. A wonderful pictorial incentive for the child to tell the story in his own words.

WHAT A TALE! by Brian Wildsmith. New York: Oxford University Press, 1981.

Another of Wildsmith's pictorial surprise endings. Each page shows an increasing number of brightly colored animal tails seemingly draped over a gate. We finally see who the animals are and where they are sitting—in a kangaroo's pouch! Splashy colors are marvelous! Nice play on tail/tale adds to the fun.

PANCAKES FOR BREAKFAST by Tomie DePaola. New York: Voyager/HBJ Book, 1978.

The delightful story of a little old lady's longing for a breakfast of pancakes told only in pictures. In spite of the missing supplies, she eventually has her pancakes, but in a most unexpected way. DePaola's pictures are endearing and even the cat and dog have the most expressive faces.

A wonderful way to entice children to tell the story themselves while "reading" the pictures.

THE KNIGHT AND THE DRAGON by Tomie De Paola. New York: Putnam's Sons, 1980.

A knight prepares to face a dangerous dragon for his very first encounter. But the dragon is anything but dangerous and both are equally inept at this momentous encounter. The side-by-side pictures of the knight reading *How to Fight Dragons* and the dragon reading *How to Fight Knights* are marvelous. The comically disastrous duel that takes place leads to a channeling of the participants' energies into something much more suited to their talents. As always, DePaola's illustrations combine the best of the comical elements.

BOOKS WITH WORDS AND PICTURES

A true picture book is created when both pictures and text are indispensable to the narrative. The book cannot stand on either the text or the pictures alone, but is a result of a skillful meshing of both. Unlike a book with illustrations that merely enhance the text, in these books the pictures are necessary for the full meaning of the story to develop. In effect, the pictures help the text to clarify the story. The following are books which have been created in this principle.

FEELINGS by Aliki. New York: Greenwillow Books, 1984.

A marvelous collection of pictures, monologues, stories, and poems depicting small children's everyday emotions ranging from very happy to very sad. Outbursts of anger and moments of fear are all treated with gentle humor but it is kindness and love that are the best feelings of all.

ROSIE'S WALK by Pat Hutchins. New York: Macmillan, 1971.

Hutchins's text consists of one long sentence (thirty-two words) that tells us about a hen called Rosie and her walk through the barnyard. What the text doesn't tell us is that Rosie is being followed by a fox who is hoping to make Rosie his supper. Poor, dumb Rosie never looks back and never knows how close she comes to becoming a hen stew. But luck is with her, for every time the fox is ready to spring, he is foiled by an uproarious piece of comedy. The real fun is in knowing what Rosie doesn't know.

DON'T FORGET THE BACON by Pat Hutchins. New York: Greenwillow Books, 1976. New York: Penguin, 1978.

A colorful trip to the store with an oral shopping list designed to tax a small boy's memory. The items change as he passes things that serve to confuse his already muddled brain. Pears become chairs, eggs become pegs and legs, until finally, as he approaches the store, it all comes back to him. Except, of course, the bacon. As usual, Pat Hutchins combines text and pictures to create literary fun.

TOM AND SAM by Pat Hutchins. New York: Puffin Books, 1972.

Best friends, Tom and Sam, enter into a competition that leads to each trying to outdo the other. Jealousy forces each to steal the other's creation and they run smack into each other trying to get away. Feigning having rescued each other's treasure from robbers, they solve their differences in a friendly way. A comical insight into the emotions involved in friendship and the desire to excel.

THE VERY WORST MONSTER by Pat Hutchins. New York: Greenwillow, 1985.

Pat Hutchins's gift allows her to create a special kind of humor. The combination of pictures and text results in a gentle, never biting humor that keeps children laughing while enjoying a delightful story. In this recent book, a family of monsters crows over the newest member of the family as the "very worst monster of all." Hazel, the big sister, sets out to prove that she, not her brother, is the very worst monster. Illustrations are nonthreatening and comical, full of bright colors.

COME AWAY FROM THE WATER, SHIRLEY by John Burningham. New York: Crowell Junior Books, 1977. New York: Harper, 1983.

A simple text with illustrations that belie the words. Therein lies the humor. Shirley and her parents spend a day at the beach. While Shirley's mother makes very commonplace comments—"Of course, it's far too cold for swimming, Shirley," and "Don't stroke that dog, Shirley, you don't know where he's been," Shirley is lost in her own imaginary world. She is on a wordless adventure, rowing out to sea, being captured by pirates, and finding buried treasure. The childlike way in which Shirley ignores her mother's chatter and embarks on her fantasy adventures will tickle every child who uses imagination to escape the everyday world.

TIME TO GET OUT OF THE BATH, SHIRLEY by John Burningham. New York: Crowell Junior Books, 1978.

While Shirley's mother talks of baths and extols the

virtues of cleanliness, Shirley slips down into the drain into a world of kings, queens, and knights. The sight of Shirley jousting from the back of her rubber duck is sure to make both parents and children giggle with delight.

MR. GUMPY'S OUTING by John Burningham. New York: Penguin, 1984.

Mr. Gumpy takes two children and an assortment of animals for a boat ride with strict "dos and don'ts." All proceed to do exactly what they were told not to do, and all, including Mr. Gumpy, get a good dunking. Abbreviated text and lovely, warm pictures enhance the machinations of the unruly passengers. By the same author—*Mr. Gumpy's Motorcar.*

WHERE'S JULIUS? by John Burningham. New York: Crown Publishers, 1986.

The magic of the imaginary life of children at play has Julius shooting the rapids in South America and riding a camel in the pyramids, all in his very own living room. Too busy to take time out for meals, Julius is fortunate enough to have accommodating parents who bring his meals to him. Wonderful little touches in each picture including a glass of pop for a thirsty camel and an orange for a hungry monkey. Bound to appeal to a child's sense of fantasy.

WOULD YOU RATHER . . . by John Burningham. New York: Crowell Junior Books, 1978.

A curly-headed little boy is offered a series of comical, improbable choices that become more and more outlandish. *Would you rather be . . . eaten by a crocodile or sat on by a rhinoceros?* The illustrations enhance the text by showing what complications can result from any of the idiotic choices. Finally, what a small boy really wants becomes his last irresistible choice. The pictorial exaggeration greatly adds to the humor.

THE SHOPPING BASKET by John Burningham. New York: Crowell Junior Books, 1980.

Steven's mother sends him shopping for a variety of items and starts him on a wonderful adventure. As he returns home with his basket full, he meets a wide assortment of animals all with one thing on their collective minds: the contents of Steven's shopping basket! Steven's mild-mannered appearance leads the animals to take aggressive action that leads to unexpected results. Another of Burningham's delightful plays on children's fantasies.

STREGA NONA by Tomie DePaola. Englewood Cliffs, N.J.: Prentice-Hall, 1975.

DePaola's humorous retelling of an old tale about "Grandma Witch," Strega Nona's magic pasta pot proves irresistible to Big Anthony who manages to get himself into a pot of trouble with it. Determined to show the townspeople how it works, Big Anthony gets it started but lacks the magic gesture to stop it. Strega Nona saves the day, and Big Anthony, when she returns. Another one of DePaola's brilliantly illustrated books.

THE TROUBLE WITH MOM by Babette Cole. New York: Putnam Publishing Group, 1984.

A young boy finds that his unusual mother has difficulty being accepted by the other parents. The trouble with Mom is that she is a witch. When Mom saves the day by putting out the school fire using her witchly powers, they are won over. The humor lies in the wonderful pictures. By the same author—*The Trouble with Dad*, and *Prince Cinders*.

MAY I BRING A FRIEND by Beatrice Schenk deRegniers. Illus. by Beni Montresor. New York: Athenium, 1964.

A lovely narrative told in verse of a boy who is repeatedly invited to tea with the king and queen. Each time he asks, "May I bring a friend?" His friends, all graciously welcomed, include giraffes, lions, and hippos among others who are not always the most mannerly. The antics of each are cleverly depicted by the wonderful, colorful illustrations.

THE STUPIDS HAVE A BALL by Harry Allard. Illus. by James Marshall. Boston: Houghton Mifflin, 1978.

The Stupids are a zany family whose name is an apt description of their actions. They celebrate when the children flunk all of their subjects and throw a costume party. The dog comes as the Bone Ranger, Grandfather Stupid comes down the chimney dressed as the Easter Bunny, carrying a pumpkin and shouting, "Ho,ho, ho!" The jokes are in the pictures as well as in the language. Guests row to the party on the grass and pictures hanging on the walls are incorrectly labeled: a flower is titled *frog*, and a pig titled *fox*. Little ones will miss some of the puns, but Mom and Dad will love them and will enjoy the bright colors and the broad exaggerated features of the characters and their surroundings. By the same authors—*The Stupids Step Out* and *The Stupids Die*.

GEORGE AND MARTHA by James Marshall. Boston: Houghton Mifflin, 1972.

Using hippos to define the meaning of friendship gives a farcical quality to these stories. George and Martha are great friends and when Martha makes pots and pots of her favorite split-pea soup for George, he doesn't have the heart to tell her he hates split-pea soup. Another story shows Martha constantly preening herself in front of the mirror and shows how George sets out to teach her the falseness of vanity. The little everyday human problems take on an absurdity as they are portrayed by two lumbering hippos. By the same author—*George and Martha Encore, George and Martha One Fine Day* and *George and Martha Rise and Shine.*

MISS NELSON IS MISSING! by Harry Allard. Illus. by James Marshall. Boston: Houghton Mifflin, 1977.

Wonderfully illustrated picture book about naughty children who drive their lovely teacher, Miss Nelson, away with their antics. In her place comes the ugly Miss Viola Swamp whose witchy appearance makes the children attend to her every word. The children's search for Miss Nelson and her triumphant return lead to a surprising and comical ending to the story. By the same author and illustrator—*Miss Nelson Is Back!*

NOSEY MRS. RAT by Jeffrey Allen and James Marshall. New York: Viking Penguin, 1985.

Shirley Rat has a peculiar hobby, snooping! She reads other people's mail, listens in on phone conversations, and peeks in windows. Her disguises don't fool her neighbors who soon tire of her shameless busybodying. But it takes Brewster Blackstone, one of the targets of Shirley's hobby, to give Shirley a taste of her own techniques. Rat family fun.

FAMILY PICTURE BOOK HUMOR

The next group finds most of its humor in family and peer relationships. Authors capture their readers with comical characters and events typical in their own lives.

STANLEY AND RHODA by Rosemary Wells. New York: Dial Press, 1978 and 1981.

Big brother Stanley watches over little sister Rhoda, a comical fuss budget who always seems to be smack in the middle of an insurmountable problem: a room to clean, a bee sting, a bath. But big brother Stanley solves them all. The contrast between Stanley's calm, orderly demeanor, and Rhoda's chaotic behavior creates much of the humor. Bright appealing pictures depict small, cuddly animals with a warm, loving mama.

BENJAMIN AND TULIP by Rosemary Wells. New York: Dial Press, 1973.

Assertive little girls will love Tulip's aggressive attacks on poor Benjamin. As if Benjamin's repeated beatings aren't enough, Aunt Fern accuses him of being at fault. Benjamin finally brings Tulip down to size, but not without some delicious antics. Wells's blending of happy illustrations and simple text uses raccoons to portray very human emotions.

BREAD AND JAM FOR FRANCES by Russell Hoban. Illus. by Lillian Hoban. New York: Harper Junior, 1964.

Frances is an endearing little girl in a badger's body who embodies all of those funny qualities that are part of a small girl's repertoire. When Frances will stubbornly eat only bread and jam, Mother uses psychology by serving her only bread and jam, while the rest of the family dines on mouth-watering meals. While at first Frances seems delighted, she soon succumbs to Mother's trick and woefully asks to be served what the rest of the family is eating. Small children (and their parents) will love Frances's funny little songs that describe exactly what she is thinking and feeling.

A BARGAIN FOR FRANCES by Russell Hoban. New York: Harper Junior, 1978.

When Frances is tricked by her friend Thelma she finds a way to turn the tables on Thelma.

A BIRTHDAY FOR FRANCES by Russell Hoban. New York: Harper Junior, 1968.

Frances is every child as she feels envious of baby sister Gloria's birthday which is fast approaching.

A BABY SISTER FOR FRANCES by Russell Hoban. New York: Harper Junior, 1964.

With the arrival of a new baby, Frances trods the path of the dethroned only child. She does everything in her power to get back what she perceives to be her lost attention. Her wise and sensitive parents succeed in giving Frances the reassurance she needs. As with all of the Frances stories, warm and gentle humor pervades the story.

BEST FRIENDS FOR FRANCES by Russell Hoban. New York: Harper Junior, 1969.

While teaching her friend Albert the meaning of friendship, Frances learns the meaning of friendship between sisters. Another humorous look at everyday events in the lives of all children.

BEDTIME FOR FRANCES by Russell Hoban. New York: Harper Junior, 1976.

Any child who has invented interminable excuses to put off bedtime will love this story. Frances runs down the list from a drink of water to a monster in her bedroom before bowing to Father's will. Although Garth Williams's Frances is a little leaner than Lillian Hoban's, she is still cuddly and endearing.

AND I MEAN IT, STANLEY by Crosby Bonsall. New York: Harper and Row, 1974.

A little boy talks to an unseen Stanley remarking that he is perfectly happy playing alone and needs no participation or company. The suspense surrounding Stanley's identity builds until the very end when a large, floppy, lovable dog leaps upon the small boy with an abundance of affection. Bound to bring a smile to a small child's face.

WHEN I GET BIGGER by Mercer Mayer. New York: Western Publishing Company, 1983.

A wonderfully comic picture book with an endearing "Little Critter" character reflecting on the realities of life and growing up. He dreams, as all children do, of the time when he will never have to be told to do anything because he will be big enough to do things on his own. By the same author—*Just Go to Bed, Me, Too!*

LYLE, LYLE, CROCODILE by Bernard Waber. Boston: Houghton-Mifflin, 1965.

A heartwarming tale of the Primm family and their unusual pet crocodile, Lyle. The humor is in the Primm's acceptance of Lyle as a member of the family and his freedom in the community. When Mrs. Primm and Lyle go shopping, Mr. Grumps, the store manager, has Lyle sent to the zoo. All's well that ends well and Lyle and the Primms are reunited. Colorful, amusing pictures complement the charming text. By the same author—*Ira Sleeps Over* and *Ira Says Goodbye*.

DINNER AT ALBERTA'S by Russell Hoban. Illus. by James Marshall. New York: Crowell Junior Books, 1975. New York: Dell, 1980.

Mr. and Mrs. Crocodile and sister Emma try to to get Arthur to clean up his act, use polite table manners, and tone down his electric guitar. But nothing helps until the day Emma brings Alberta home for dinner. Arthur is smitten, and when Alberta invites him to her house for dinner, he sets out to be a model of cleanliness and courtesy. Children will love this warm, funny story of a very human crocodile family.

LENGTHY by Syd Hoff. New York: Putnam Publishing Group, 1979.

Hoff's familiar cartoon-style illustrations tell the story of Lengthy, the dachshund who is so long he cannot see his own tail. His adventures lead him to run away to the home of a very rich family where he foils an attempted robbery. Tired of the easy life, Lengthy returns home to a royal welcome.

I'LL FIX ANTHONY by Judith Viorst. Illus. by Arnold Lobel. New York: Harper and Row, 1969.

Sibling rivalry creates comical talk and thoughts of a little brother. He lists all of the things he will be able to do when he is six and so surpass Anthony. All children will relate to the "when I grow up" theme. By the same author—*Alexander and the Terrible, Horrible, No Good, Very Bad Day.*

HARRY'S DOG by Barbara Ann Porte. Illus. by Yossi Abolafia. New York: Greenwillow, 1984.

Harry's father is allergic to dogs and Harry's attempt to keep his dog, Girl, hidden are a riot. He hides her in the least expected places, but, alas, Harry's father sneezes away so Girl is uncovered. The problem is finally solved by letting Girl live nearby at the home of Harry's aunt.

Will appeal to all children who have or long for a pet. By the same author—*Harry's Mom* and *Harry's Visit*.

HARRY THE DIRTY DOG by Gene Zion. Illus. by Margaret Bloy Graham. New York: Harper Junior, 1956.

Harry's endearing qualities lie in his ability to get into doggylike scrapes which often take him out of the safety of his home and into the large, rather comical, world. In this story, Harry slides down a coal chute and is transformed "from a white dog with black spots to a black dog with white spots." Harry's hidden identity makes for humorous misadventures. By the same author—*No Roses for Harry* and *Harry by the Sea*.

FROG AND TOAD ARE FRIENDS by Arnold Lobel. New York: Harper and Row, 1970. New York: Harper Junior, 1979.

Another peek at the trials and tribulations of friendship using two irresistible amphibian friends. Frog and Toad help each other out with cheerful good humor. One of the funniest episodes occurs in "The Swim" when Toad remains in the river in order to hide his bathing suit from the other animals. Lobel's illustrations are classicallly funny. By the same author—*Frog and Toad All Year*, *Frog and Toad Together*, and *Days with Frog and Toad*.

HARRIET'S RECITAL by Nancy Carlson. New York: Penguin, 1985.

Harriet is every little girl who has ever been terrified of her first ballet recital. What makes Harriet's plight laughable is the fact that Harriet is a dog. Using animals to depict children's feelings never fails to delight a child and Harriet's worries about her costume ripping and forgetting her dance steps is a howling success. By the same author—*Harriet and the Garden* and *Harriet and the Roller Coaster*.

JACOB TWO-TWO MEETS THE HOODED FANG by Mordecai Richler. Illus. by Fritz Wegner. New York: Bantam-Skylark (Dell), 1987.

Beware the horrible, disgusting, mean, vicious, evil, and vile Hooded Fang who runs the children's prison where Jacob Two-Two is sent for the terrible crime of insulting a grown-up. Jacob and the other children are forced to make rain for picnics, no-flow ketchup, and jigsaw puzzles too complicated to solve. But Jacob finds the way to disarm the Hooded Fang and frees all of the children. Wonderfully funny fantasy that will appeal to a child's love of horror tales.

THE SHRINKING OF TREEHORN by Florence Parry Heide. Illus. by Edward Gorey. New York: Holiday House, 1971. New York: Penguin/Puffin, 1975.

Grown-ups who never seem to listen to what a child is saying are the focus of the humor in Treehorn. Treehorn is shrinking and no one hears his plaintive plea. When the adults in his world finally realize that he is shrinking, they do absolutely nothing to help. A classic bit of nonsense designed to make children giggle at the absentminded behavior of adults.

TREEHORN'S TREASURE by Florence Parry Heide. Illus. by Edward Gorey. New York: Holiday House, 1981. New York: Penguin/Puffin, 1984.

More fun with adults who refuse to listen when a child speaks. Treehorn discovers money growing on a tree in his backyard and, you guessed it, no one believes him. A delightful romp through every child's fondest fantasy.

TREEHORN'S WISH by Florence Parry Heide. Illus. by Edward Gorey. New York: Holiday House, 1984.
Treehorn finds a jug with a genie inside which leads to a hilarious set of misunderstandings.

A CHOCOLATE MOOSE FOR DINNER by Fred Gwynne. New York: Windmill Books and E.P. Dutton Company, 1976.
The wonderful story of a little girl who takes everything her parents say literally. The pictures show the child's literal interpretations, so when Daddy says he has "trees for his shoes," the picture shows an actual tree with shoes all over it. This is a kind of visual *Amelia Bedelia*. By the same author—*The King Who Rained*.

THE DAY THE TEACHER WENT BANANAS by James Howe. Illus. by Lillian Hoban. New York: E. P. Dutton, 1984.
The humorous situation of having a gorilla as a teacher for a day will delight children. The bright and colorful illustrations complement the outrageous antics of the children as they experience a decidedly different day at school.

FLAT STANLEY by Jeff Brown. Illus. by Tomi Ungerer. New York: Harper Junior, 1964.
When the bulletin board beside his bed flattens him to a half-inch thick, Stanley Lambchop takes full advantage of the experience. He squeezes under doors, slides between the bars of a sidewalk grate, and is even mailed to California

in an envelope. Brown's comical text coupled with Ungerer's whimsical pictures make this book a delight.

A LAMP FOR THE LAMBCHOPS by Jeff Brown. Illus. by Lynn Wheeling. New York: Harper and Row, 1983.

In the prologue, we find that the Genie King has sentenced Prince Haraz to lamp duty for playing too many jokes in the kingdom. Stanley finds an old metal teapot on the beach and when he rubs it, a genie, alias Prince Haraz, appears. Jeff Browns plays with the old against the new when he supplies the genie with an answer basket that gives a recorded message when all the genies are busy. The fun centers around Stanely's wishes and Mr. and Mrs. Lambchop's calm acceptance of the genie. The juxtaposition of fantasy and realism is wonderful.

THE ENORMOUS CROCODILE by Roald Dahl. Illus. by Quentin Blake. New York: Alfred A. Knopf Company, 1978.

A delicious story about a mean, ugly crocodile who sets out to trap unsuspecting little boys and girls. But the crocodile didn't count on the other jungle animals who foil him at every turn, proving once again that good will triumphs over evil. Designed to give children and their parents a wonderful giggle.

ARTHUR'S EYES by Marc Brown. New York: Avon Books, 1979.

When Arthur's poor eyesight forces him to get glasses, the results are predictable. His friends laugh at him and call him names until Arthur decides to "lose" his glasses. But a sensitive and perceptive teacher shows Arthur how to wear his glasses with style. A humorous look at a very common problem. As in many picture books for children, the use of animals as the characters makes the situations even funnier.

DOCTOR DESOTO by William Steig. New York: Scholastic, 1984.

Doctor DeSoto, the dentist, is a mouse who treats all animals, large and small, except those who might be dangerous to him and his assistant, who happens to be his wife. However, one day, he succumbs to the pleas of a fox in great pain and agrees to treat his aching tooth. The offending tooth is pulled and the doctor makes an appointment to fit a brand new tooth in the fox's mouth. The fox, however, shows his foxy colors and begins to think about a mouse supper. But never fear, Doctor DeSoto outfoxes the fox by sealing his jaws shut. A comical tale of animal antics.

PADDINGTON HELPS OUT by Michael Bond. New York: Dell, 1970.

Paddington is one of those wonderful characters who combines animal and human characteristics in the best possible way. What Michael Bond counts on is the sharing of the fun of an animal who speaks and acts like a human and combines a kind of adult/child existence. As an adult, Paddington is free to come and go as he pleases, yet it is this very freedom that constantly gets him into trouble. He floods the laundry room, bids at an auction sale, and creates havoc in the kitchen. All of the Paddington books are fun, but this is one of my favorites.

OLGA CARRIES ON by Michael Bond. New York: Dell, 1983.

Olga, the guinea pig, climbs new heights as she raises

the alarm when she sees smoke coming from the house, solves a mystery, and writes a poem. Each chapter is a complete story. Olga has the same gentle humor of Bond's Paddington Bear.

IMOGENE'S ANTLERS by David Small. New York: Crown Publishers, 1985.

When Imogene awakens to find antlers growing out of her head, the reactions of her family and friends are comically diverse. Mother faints, the principal glares, and brother Norman reads the encyclopedia and announces that Imogene has turned into a miniature elk. The most practical reactions come from the domestic staff who use the antlers to dry towels and to feed doughnuts to the birds in the garden. The antlers disappear one morning only to be replaced by, oops, you'll have to read it to find out! A zany romp through a delicious tale.

REALISTIC PICTURE BOOKS

FIRST GRADE TAKES A TEST by Miriam Cohen. Illus. by Lillian Hoban. New York: Dell, 1980.

A gently humorous little book showing how taking standardized tests can worry small children. Finding the right answers is not easy for everyone and sometimes there doesn't seem to be any right answer. Who is the smartest one in the class and is that really what is important? Cohen touches on the very real problem of testing for small children and manages to make it all come out all right. By the same author and illustrator—*No Good in Art, When Will I Read?*, and *Lost in the Museum*.

THE ONE IN THE MIDDLE IS THE GREEN KANGAROO by Judy Blume. New York: Dell, 1982.

Perennial problem of the "middle child" who feels caught between big brother and baby sister. Finally, Freddie has a chance to show his stuff in the school play. Blume always handles children's problems with compassion and humor.

ECLECTIC PICTURE BOOKS

WHO WANTS A CHEAP RHINOCEROS? by Shel Silverstein. New York: Macmillan, 1983.

By now, the playful works of Shel Silverstein are famous, and this tale is one of his funniest. Singing the praises of this unusual pet, the author takes us on a romp through the variety of positive qualities that the rhino exhibits and a few negative ones as well. Silverstein's ability to use black and white line drawings to convey humor, action, and emotion is brillant. This is one of those ageless books to cherish. By the same author—*A Giraffe and a Half.*

THE JOLLY POSTMAN by Janet and Allan Ahlberg. Boston: Little Brown, 1986.

The Ahlbergs have written an ingenious book that combines a giggle with a look at a variety of correspondence. Fairytale characters write letters to each other and others, and each letter or postcard is actually in the book in its own envelope. Little fingers can remove each letter and enjoy the childlike writing that appears. Parents will love the letter from a lawyer to the Big Bad Wolf threatening him with a lawsuit. This is the kind of book that will please children at one level and parents at another. Sure to bring many hours of fun.

FUNNYBONES by Janet and Allan Ahlberg. New York: Greenwillow, 1980.

The Funnybones are skeletons who go out to scare people. Since there is no one around to frighten, they proceed to frighten each other. Their trip through the town leads them to the zoo where they cavort with the animal skeletons. The skeletons are smiling and nonthreatening and the children will love the repetitions in the text. By the same author—*The Ha Ha Bonk Book*.

AMELIA BEDELIA by Peggy Parish. Illus. by Fritz Siebel. New York: Harper Junior, 1963.

Amelia Bedelia takes everything that is said literally, so when Mrs. Rogers tells her to dress the chicken she does just that—with socks and green shorts. Her day is spent busily doing as she is told but not exactly as it was meant. But before her actions cause her to lose her job, her employers taste her lemon meringue pie! Mmmm! A wonderful way to have fun and learn the fun of language and its multiple meanings.

HUGE HAROLD by Bill Peet. Boston: Houghton Mifflin, 1961.

A tiny rabbit turns into a giant causing all kinds of funny and dangerous consequences. It is only when he ends up on Orville B. Croft's farm that he becomes a real racy rabbit (champion trotter that is).

THE KWEEKS OF KOOKATUMDEE by Bill Peet. Boston: Houghton Mifflin, 1958.

Birdlike Kweeks are starving for lack of ploppolop fruit

to feed them until Quentin takes on Jed, the greedy Kweek, and learns how to fly.

Fantasy, Textual Humor—Ages 8–11

Fantasy happens when the bounds of reality are broken and disbelief is suspended.* Characters and their actions become fanciful when the way they look, act, or speak cannot happen in the real world as we know it. The wide range of modern humorous fantasies offers children many trips through magical situations with zany, improbable characters.

Books of fantasy include those set in mythical places and those with realistic settings. Characters in mythical settings may be realistic (Alice in Wonderland, Milo in *The Phantom Tollbooth*) and realistic settings may have make-believe characters (*Pippi Longstocking, The Hoboken Chicken Emergency*). The qualifying characteristic of a fantasy is the inability of the story to really happen. That is the factor that takes the story beyond the bounds of realism. The collection of books listed in this section embraces all levels of fantasy treated with deft touches of humor.

THE TWITS by Roald Dahl. Illus. by Quentin Blake. New York: Penguin/Puffin, 1982.

Putting Roald Dahl and Quentin Blake together creates the absolute best in humor in story and pictures. They are

---

*Rebecca Lukens, *A Critical Handbook of Children's Literature* (Greenview, Il.: Scott Foresman, 1976).

an unbeatable combination. There's not a child who will not howl at the incredibly nasty, ugly, heartless Twits. The loathsome couple play evil tricks on each other, the birds, the monkeys, and anyone else who comes into their line of vision. But the Muggle-Wump monkeys and the Roly-Poly bird finally beat them at their own nasty game and give the Twits an ending they richly deserve.

THE BFG by Roald Dahl. Illus. by Quentin Blake. New York: Penguin, 1985.

A Dahlesque tall tale of a Big Friendly Giant who cannot speak English because he has never been to school. He and his friend Sophie, "a human bean," plot the destruction of the evil giants, Childchewer, Bonecrusher, and Maidmasher. Another triumph by Dahl and Blake.

THE GIRAFFE & THE PELLY & ME by Roald Dahl. Illus. by Quentin Blake. New York: Penguin, 1987.

An absurdly delicious tale about a small boy's adventure with a giraffe, a pelican, and a monkey. The animals, who are a very unusual windowwashing team, take part in the capture of a dangerous burglar on the estate of the Duke of Hampshire. Another winning brainchild by Dahl and Blake.

THE WITCHES by Roald Dahl. Illus. by Quentin Blake. New York: Penguin, 1985.

"Real witches dress in ordinary clothes and look very much like ordinary women." How's a child to know? Is it your neighbor? Or, heaven forbid, your teacher? Dahl sets out to help you recognize one. They are bald, always wear gloves, and spit blue. Wonderful, improbable tales of the narrator's wild escapades with witches. The illustrations are hilarious!

BANANA TWIST by Florence Parry Heide. New York: Holiday House, 1978. New York: Bantam-Skylark (Dell), 1987.

The comic story of Jonah D. Crock's attempts to elude his oddball neighbor, Goober, who is convinced that Jonah has a banana fixation. Goober follows Jonah everywhere and succeeds in making Jonah anxious to escape to Fairlee School where every room has a TV and a refrigerator. Hilarious! By the same author—*Banana Blitz* and *At School with Jonah and Goober*.

RUNAWAY RALPH by Beverly Cleary. Illus. by Louis Darling. New York: Morrow, 1970. New York: Dell, 1981.

Tale of a motorcycle-riding mouse named Ralph, who is the bane of his family's existence. Ralph runs away to Happy Acres Camp, is almost eaten by a family of cats and is rescued by Garf, the hamster. Ralph's daring escape shows Catso, the cat, as the real villain. Wonderful, fanciful tale of an incorrigible mouse.

THE CELERY STALKS AT MIDNIGHT by James Howe. Illus. by Leslie Morrill. New York: Atheneum, 1983.

This sequel to the popular *Bunnicula* is as funny as the original. Bunnicula, the missing vegetable vampire, sparks a search led by Chester, the cat, for vegetables that Bunnicula has turned into vampires. Delightful characters seen in improbably funny situations. By the same author—*Howliday Inn*.

THE ENORMOUS EGG by Oliver Butterworth. Illus. by Louis Darling. Boston: Little, Brown and Company, 1956. New York: Dell, 1978.

The enormous egg laid by a hen belonging to the Twitchell family is the start of a fancifully funny story. The egg hatches and a dinosaur emerges and with it a series of problems. Its rapid growth makes feeding impossible and it is shipped to the National Zoo. The dinosaur gets national attention and leads to a bill banning dinosaurs. Wonderful use of fantasy in a realistic setting.

MAMA DON'T ALLOW by Thatcher Hurd. New York: Harper Junior, 1984.

Miles Possum and the Swamp Band love playing at the Alligator Ball until they discover that they are on the menu. The band's quick decision to play "Lullaby of Swampland," which puts the alligators to sleep, saves them. Marvelous, colorful pictures.

PIPPI LONGSTOCKING by Astrid Lindgren. Illus. by Louis S. Glanzman. New York: Penguin, 1977.

An improbable fantasy in which eight-year-old Pippi lives all alone in a little house in a tiny town. Well not exactly alone, however, for living with her are Mr. Nilsson, the monkey, and Horse, but no adults are in evidence. Pippi does exactly as she pleases so she stays up late, eats whenever she's hungry, and goes to school only so that she can have a Christmas vacation. Pippi's unusual appearance plus her outlandish feats make her an appealing character. Other adventures of Pippi—*Pippi Goes on Board* and *Pippi in the South Seas*.

THE GENIE OF SUTTON PLACE by George Selden. New York: Farrar, Straus and Giroux, 1973.

The discovery of an ancient Arabic spell for calling forth a genie changes Tim Farr's life. When his Aunt Lucy insists that he get rid of his dog, Sam, Tim is desperate Abdullah, disguised as Aunt Lucy's chauffeur, changes Sam into a man, and there begins an engaging tale of a man who cannot get the dog out of him, a genie let out of a rug and an unusual boy who loves the occult. A marvelous meshing of wit, fantasy and incongruous characters.

JENNIFER, HECATE, MACBETH, WILLIAM MCKINLEY, AND ME, ELIZABETH by E. L. Konigsburg. New York: Atheneum, 1967.

Elizabeth stops being the loneliest child in the United States when she becomes Jennifer's apprentice witch. Much to her surprise, she learns to eat raw eggs, cast short spells and, best of all, to get along with Jennifer. Elizabeth escapes into Jennifer's fantasy world where she finds a real friend. Elizabeth has no more time to be lonely as she and Jennifer have crazy and wonderful adventures. Konigsburg is a master storyteller who catches every child with her sense of fantasy. It is difficult to tell where the fantasy ends and the real world begins. By the same author—*From the Mixed-Up Files of Mrs. Basil E. Frankweiler.*

THE HOBOKEN CHICKEN EMERGENCY by Manus M. Pinkwater. New York: Scholastic, 1978.

A hilarious tall tale that begins with a little boy's search for a Thanksgiving turkey which leads to a 266-pound chicken named Henrietta. The chicken becomes a pet and the trials of keeping her make for hilarious reading. The text is enhanced by wonderful black and white drawings that illustrate the humor of the text.

THE PHANTOM TOLLBOOTH by Norton Juster. New York: Random House, 1961.

When Milo begins his journey through Dictionopolis and Digitopolis, we are treated to a modern day trip through Wonderland. Milo and the dog, Tock, meet a bizarre assortment of characters as they move through a story laced with verbal puns and jokes. Young children will enjoy the fun of the journey and older children and parents will delight in the stunning use of words and numbers. The only book for children based on verbal humor since *Alice*.

Realism—Ages 8 and Up

Realistic fiction takes a character and situations from everyday life and presents them in a representation of the child's own world. Subject matter covers relationships with parents, siblings, friends, teachers, and neighbors. When an author tells the story highlighting the humor found in everyday situations, the child is able to see that what may appear so serious to him/her is common to most children.

HELP! THERE'S A CAT WASHING IN HERE! by Allison Smith. Illus. by Amy Rowen. New York: Dutton, 1981.
   Wonderfully funny story of twelve-year-old Henry Walker and his family. When Henry's mother needs uninterrupted time to prepare an art portfolio for a job application, Henry takes charge of the household chores, including his brother Joe and his little sister Annie. Anything to avoid asking bossy Aunt Wilhelmina to move in. Things are difficult enough, but with Annie's friend, the neighborhood terror, and Annie's big, frightening black cat complicating things, Henry almost reaches the end of his patience. Giggles galore!

THE EIGHTEENTH EMERGENCY by Betsy Byars. Illus. by Robert Grossman. New York: Viking, 1973. New York: Penguin/Puffin Books, 1976.
   Benjie and his friend Ezzie know just what to do when

attacked by a werewolf or approached by a crocodile, but when facing a hammering from Marvin Hammerman, the biggest, toughest boy in the school, they are just plain scared. Anyone who has ever faced the school bully will sympathize and laugh with Benjie as he faces his biggest emergency yet. By the same author—*The TV Kid* and *The Computer Nut*.

TALES OF A FOURTH GRADE NOTHING by Judy Blume. New York: Dutton, 1972. New York: Dell, 1986.

An older brother or sister will sympathize with Peter's trials with little brother Fudge. Peter feels like a "nothing" when no one, especially his parents, understands his problems. Although Fudge is an unholy terror with willful behavior and lack of respect for everyone's possessions, especially Peter's, he continues to be in firm control of the household. A hilarious combination of improbable episodes coupled with a real understanding of the child's viewpoint make a winning combination.

SUPERFUDGE by Judy Blume. New York: Dell, 1981.

A continuation of Peter's problems with Fudge. A new twist is added when Mrs. Hatcher tells Peter there will soon be a new little Hatcher. Oh no! Fudge II!

RAMONA THE PEST by Beverly Cleary. New York: Dell, 1982.

Like Fudge, Ramona presents a problem for her older sister Beezus. Ramona isn't really a pest but a normal, inquisitive little girl with a million questions and the logic of a five-year-old. Not really for small children, but their older brothers and sisters who will recognize Ramona immediately. By the same author—*Ramona Quimby Age 8*, *Ramona the Brave* and *Beezus and Ramona*.

ISABELLE THE ITCH by Constance C. Greene. New York: Viking, 1973. New York: Dell, 1987.

Any parent who has ever had an itchy child and every child who has ever itched will love Isabelle. Isabelle is bursting with energy that she cannot control and she drives everyone around her slightly mad. When Isabelle gets a chance to deliver her brother's papers for a week, she meets Mrs. Stern, who helps her see how to channel her overabundant energy into positive accomplishments, much to Isabelle's delight. Greene's characters are both warm and humorous and refreshingly real. By the same author—*The Unmasking of Rabbit*.

ANASTASIA AGAIN by Lois Lowry. Illus. by Diane DeGroat Boston: Houghton Mifflin, 1981. New York: Dell, 1982.

Lively, appealing Anastasia returns as her family moves to the suburbs amidst Anastasia's misgivings. Developing new friendships and meeting new people help Anastasia overcome her prejudice toward suburban folk. The humor is in both character and dialogue. By the same author—*Anastasia, Ask Your Analyst* and *Anastasia at Your Service*.

ORDINARY JACK by Helen Cresswell. New York: Macmillan, 1977. New York: Avon, 1979.

What happens when the only ordinary member of a talented family decides to excel at something in order to gain his share of attention? Jack amazes the whole family when he acquires strange and mysterious powers.

Cresswell's sparkling dialogue and eccentric characters are sure to please. By the same author—*Absolute Zero*.

DOES THIS SCHOOL HAVE CAPITAL PUNISHMENT? by Nat Hentoff. New York: Delacorte Press, 1981. New York: Dell, 1983.

Sam Davidson has had a checkered career at school and his retention at Burr Academy depends upon his ability to control his behavior. But Sam soon faces trouble once again and it takes all the help of his friend, jazz musician Major Kelley, to set everything right. The relationship between Sam and the Major is filled with affection and respect and a large dose of humor.

HARRIET THE SPY by Louise Fitzhugh. New York: Dell, 1985.

Harriet is in training to become a writer and she does it by writing down everything she sees and thinks in a little notebook that she carries around with her. The trouble is she is unfailingly honest in her views and spares no one. When curious classmates steal her notebook and read it, they are furious! Harriet's humorous observations about the people in her life are not funny to those she has ridiculed. Harriet eventually solves her problems and turns her comical observations into a class newspaper. A very funny portrait of a lonely child.

HOMER PRICE by Robert McCloskey. New York: Scholastic Books, 1968.

Episodes about a small town boy who always finds himself at the center of some unbelievable situation. Surrounded by incompetent, distracted adults, Homer usually saves the town from some minor disaster. The funniest and the most famous is the doughnut machine that will not stop making doughnuts. An old favorite that still delights the young readers.

DEAR MR. HENSHAW by Beverly Cleary. Illus. by Paul O. Zelinsky. New York: Dell, 1983.

This Newbery Award winner is very special. Leigh Botts, a rather lonely fifth grader, tells the story of his life through letters to an author whose books he likes to read. With warm and compassionate humor, Cleary shows us how the pain of his parents' divorce has colored Leigh's life. This is a very contemporary book about very real problems.

Fantasy for Older Children—8 and Up

This section includes a variety of fantasies, some picture books and some depending on textual humor. Age is difficult to recommend in this group since much will depend on the child's reading experience and sense of humor. I would not recommend any of these books for children under eight since they will miss much of the author's humor. Parents will love all of these and undoubtedly find much more to laugh at than their children will.

FREAKY FRIDAY by Mary Rodgers. New York: Harper and Row, 1972.

It isn't every mother who can switch bodies with her daughter to let her in on what it's like to be the mother of a teenager, but that's exactly what Mrs. Andrews does. What results is a revealing day for Annabel as she slides from one near calamity to another. This is a tale designed to charm girls and their mothers as they see the laughable side of the generation gap.

A BILLION FOR BORIS by Mary Rodgers. New York: Harper Junior, 1976.

This story continues the saga of Annabel Andrews, her brother Ape Face, and Boris Harris, Annabel's down-to-earth boyfriend. In a fascinating blend of fantasy and realism, Ape Face takes a TV set that is beyond repair and gets it to do something it never did before—broadcast tomorrow's programs! How Annabel and Boris decide to use this magical box leads to a series of improbable and madcap adventures designed to keep everyone laughing. Much of the humor lies in the way in which Annabel and Boris deal with the frightfully predictable adults in their lives.

TALES FOR THE PERFECT CHILD by Florence Parry Heide. Illus. by Victoria Chess. New York: Lee and Shepherd Lothrop, 1985.

Stories of children with less than the best behavior that is masked by sly actions and misleading words. A parade of deliciously wicked characters moves through very funny stories about children whom we all recognize. Fun for parents and children sharing the humor and love in growing up.

ALICE'S ADVENTURES IN WONDERLAND AND THROUGH THE LOOKING GLASS by Lewis Carroll. Variety of copies available in paperback.

Alice appeals to all ages with its outlandish characters and improbable plays on words. Children laugh at the story and the wonderful rhymes without worrying about the layers of social and political criticism involved. Older children and adults can return to *Alice* again and again, never getting all of Carroll's literary jokes in one or more readings. A wonderful read aloud for parent and child.

Parody

Stories featuring normally frightening characters as benign and nonthreatening are an unexpected source of humor. Older children recognize the humor in the timid fox, the friendly witch, and the nervous ghost. These stories are often parodies of old and familiar stories that delight children in their new, comical setting. Numerous authors use this form to mimic the style and content of some of our most famous literary characters.

FABLES by Arnold Lobel. New York: Harper and Row, 1980.

Lobel's text and illustrations parody the traditional fable form with high humor. The variety of animal characters just happen to remind you of lots of people that you know. Often the parents are stranger than the children and when the school principal comes to complain about the children's behavior in "The Bad Kangaroo," he finds the parents more mischievous than the children. The morals speak to the vanity and greed of people. Wonderfully comical!

REVOLTING RHYMES by Roald Dahl. Illus. by Quentin Blake. New York: Alfred A. Knopf Company, 1983.

A delicious parody of some of your favorite fairy tales told in outrageous rhyme. Red Riding Hood exchanges her cloak of red for a "lovely, furry Wolfskin coat." And what does Red Riding Hood acquire when one of the Three

Little Pigs calls her for help in fighting the wolf? A "Pigskin Traveling Case!" Keep this one away from the little ones!

DIRTY BEASTS by Roald Dahl. Illus. by Quentin Blake. New York: Penguin, 1983.

Another bit of rhymed nonsense about a cow who flies, an anteater who eats aunts, and a tummy that actually talks! Dahl's wicked humor and Blake's outlandish pictures are sidesplitting. Not for the very young.

MORE FUN WITH DICK AND JANE by Marc Gregory Gallant. New York: Penguin, 1986.

Parents who remember the Dick and Jane readers will howl at this Yuppie version. Dick and Susan are married and have their own children and Jane is selling Amway, while Sally is into aerobics. The format, including the pictures, is an exact replica of the early readers. Children and parents can laugh together at this hilarious parody.

PAT THE YUPPIE by Jim Becker and Ann Mayer. New York: Perigee Books, 1986.

Remember when the kids were reading *Pat the Bunny*? Well, now there is a perfect parody using those news-making Yuppies as the characters. So we are treated to a touch of the wonderful BMW seat covers, the pasta in the pasta machine, and even the bricks in the new condo. The format is exactly the same as the original allowing older children to make the comparison easily. A wonderful spoof of what some people think is important today.

JIM AND THE BEANSTALK by Raymond Briggs. New York: Penguin, 1980.

Our old friend Jack, masquerading as Jim, climbs up the beanstalk to find quite a different kind of giant. He is old, toothless, bald, and can't see very well. Needless to say, he doesn't present much of a threat. But Jim, unlike Jack, has no larceny on his mind and sets out to make life more tolerable for the giant. He fixes him up with a huge set of false teeth, the biggest pair of eyeglasses ever made, and a red, curly wig. When the giant can see and chew his appetite returns and Jim doesn't wait around to see if he becomes the giant's dinner. Surprise ending in keeping with the rest of the giant's benign behavior. A fun spoof of an old, familiar fairy tale.

THE BUTTER BATTLE BOOK by Dr. Seuss. New York: Random House, 1984.

With his comical verse and inventive drawings, Dr. Seuss exposes the folly of the arms race. Portraying the battle between the Yooks and the Zooks and its escalation, we are exposed to each new weapon from slingshots to the most elaborate automatic device until both sides invent the ultimate weapon: the bomb. A departure for Dr. Seuss and a wonderful way to explain the arms race to children. It is made very clear that no one can win. By the same author—*You're Only Old Once*.

THE PRINCESS AND THE FROG by A. Vesey. New York: Methuen Children's Books, 1985.

Hilarious takeoff on the familiar fairy tale setting in which the kind and loving frog is kissed by the beautiful princess and turns into a handsome prince. This frog is pushy, greedy and grumpy. But the queen, believing the old fairy tale, insists that they treat the frog well and grant his every wish. When the princess finally takes courage and kisses the miserable frog, no prince appears, and the frog gives a reasonable and sensible explanation. Another in a growing collection of parodies for children.

THE THREE NAUGHTY SISTERS MEET BLUEBEARD by R. Capdevila. Illus. by M. Company. English version by Marily Malin. New York: Methuen Children's Books, 1986.

Original peek at a traditional Perrault fairy tale in which the Wicked Witch sends triplet sisters into Storybookland as punishment for their naughty actions. But plans go awry as the sisters escape from Bluebeard and the Witch herself. Lively text and illustrations plus an entertaining game at the story's end make this a treat for youngsters.

PRINCESS SMARTYPANTS by Babette Cole. New York: Putnam Publishing Group, 1987.

Using the traditional fairy tale format, Cole turns the story of the king who seeks a husband for his daughter, the princess, into a sidesplitting version designed to tickle the entire family. This modern day princess wants no part of men and finds impossible tasks for each prospective suitor to fulfill. When one young gentleman performs the impossible, the princess makes him wish he had remained at home. A new twist on the frog who was a prince.

UNCLE SHELBY'S ABZ by Shel Silverstein. New York: Simon and Schuster, Inc., 1985.

Don't let the little ones near this one! A howl of a takeoff on the scores of ABC books for youngsters that takes the unspeakable and speaks it all. The conventional cover appears to contain the usual ABC, but a peek at the first few pages soon dispels any such thoughts. Bound to delight Mom, Dad, and the older siblings.

CLEVER POLLY AND THE STUPID WOLF by Catherine Storr. New York: Penguin/Puffin, 1984.

A wonderful collection of vignettes of a transformed

Red Riding Hood and her adversary, the wolf. This young lady is strong and crafty while the wolf is weak and easily fooled. Poor wolf has read the original version and can't quite understand why he can't get Polly to react the same way. The fun is in Polly's seemingly innocent demeanor and the wolf's nonplussed reactions.

Picture Books for Older Children—Ages 9–13

This section will include books using the comic strip format that seems to capture the attention of so many children. We have all come to know and love the *Peanuts* books and eagerly snap up any new collection of the daily strips. But there are other marvelous collections by wise authors who capture the young reader with the format they love best. The combination of words and pictures communicates the stories more fully than words alone. The nine to thirteen year old is the crucial group to entice into books since the world of television is a major part of their lives. In the hands of artist/authors, there is no more exciting format than the comic strip narrative. Reading any one of the following books will instantly dispel the notion that picture books are for only the very young.

RAYMOND BRIGGS

Our deepest thanks should go to Great Britain for the gift of Raymond Briggs. Briggs is really ageless in his readership, which is probably why readers of all ages, from kindergartners to grandparents, are drawn to his books. Many of his works are social criticisms of the class system in Great Britain, yet he manages to approach it all with humor and warmth.

FATHER CHRISTMAS by Raymond Briggs. New York: Putnam Publishing Group, 1973. New York: Penguin, 1977.
 A incongruously grumpy Santa complains about the weather, his busy Christmas Eve and life in general. His journey takes him to farmhouses, palaces, city houses, apartments, and even igloos. (How do you get into this thing?) He's terribly glad to escape the ice and snow and return to the warmth of his cozy kitchen. This Santa, unlike the one we all imagine, stomps around bemoaning his job and his gifts ("Blooming awful tie . . . "). The artwork is marvelous! Each frame is a wonder with details correct down to the tiniest item. This is a comic book! By the same author—*Father Christmas Goes on Holiday*.

ASTERIX THE GAUL by Goscinny. Illus. by Uderzo. Canada: Darguad, 1984.
 Everyone loves a pun and this French-originated cartoon series is full of them. One is amazed at how the translation from the French is able to retain the punning, including such names as Getafix the Druid and Vitalstatistix the chief. Themes are broad and appealing with the underdog prevailing and the pictures full of comical exaggerations. No offense can be taken since nearly every race comes in for a touch of gentle humor. Younger children will miss much of the verbal fun, but older children and adults will revel in the language play. By the same author—*Asterix and the Great Crossing*.

THE ADVENTURES OF TINTIN IN AMERICA by Herge. Boston: Atlantic-Little, Brown, 1979.
 Tintin, world reporter #1, with his talking dog Snowy, travels the globe cleaning up crime. In this episode, he encounters Chicago mobsters, hostile Indians, is kid-

napped, thrown in a dungeon and endures all kinds of fatal escapades until he proves, once again that "crime doesn't pay." The tongue-in-cheek humor and cartoon format will appeal to children who can appreciate the fun in exaggeration and parody. Although the characters are stereotyped, they are amazingly human. Tintin, himself, is every child's dream. There are no parents in sight, he doesn't have to go to school, and travels all over the world without seeming to worry about about getting the money for foreign travel. One of a whole series of books about Tintin.

Jokes, Limericks, and Zany Poetry—All Ages

YOUR BURRO IS NO JACKASS by Jim Aylward. Illus. by Laura Hartman. New York: Avon, 1981.

A curious collection of unusual facts and information that one might never expect to find available. Contains the latest comical facts about dandelions, goats, hiccups, and snails. "The artificial sweetner, Saccharine, is just over 100 years old. Happy birthday, sweetie!"

THE HA HA BONK BOOK by Allan and Janet Ahlberg. New York: Penguin, 1982.

Wonderful collection of riddles, jokes and funny stories, including jokes for mom, dad, baby brother, teacher, and even the dog. Many are accompanied by comical little line drawings including one of a door saying, "I hate these knock knock jokes." "What do you get when you cross an owl with a skunk? A bird that smells but doesn't give a hoot!"

NUTTY KNOCK KNOCKS by Joseph Rosenbloom. Illus. by Sandy Hoffman. New York: Sterling Publishing, 1986.

A collection of new and different knock knocks designed to tickle "Knock knock" lovers everywhere. Every child can be the life of the party with this alphabetically arranged group of jokes guaranteed to earn howls and screams. "Knock knock. Who's there? Demand. Demand who? Demand from U.N.C.L.E."

MONSTER KNOCK KNOCKS by William Cole. Illus. by Mike Thaler. New York: Archway, 1982.

Another collection of children's favorites. It's a mystery why these jokes continue to delight generation after generation of children, but the continual publishing of more and more knock knocks proves it to be so. "Knock knock. Who's there? Dakota. Dakota who? Dakota fit fine but da pants-a too big."

THE WIT AND WISDOM OF FAT ALBERT by Bill Cosby. Illus. by Filmation. Boston: Windmill Books and E. P. Dutton, 1973.

Full of funny sayings that somehow sound like something Cosby might have said. "Stop crime in the streets—stay home." "Church is where you go on Sunday to see who didn't."

GUNGA, YOUR DIN-DIN IS READY by Ray Doty. Garden City, N.Y.: Doubleday, 1976.

Puns, jokes, gags, and riddles designed to make children of all ages giggle. Lots of plays on words. "Baby teeth are dropouts!" "Suppose you crossed King Kong with Godzilla. What would you have? A heart attack." "What is a polygon? A dead parrot." By the same author—*Puns, Gags, Quips and Riddles* and *Q's Are Weird O's*.

BALLPOINT BANANAS by Charles Keller. Illus. by David Barris. Englewood Cliffs, N.J.: Prentice-Hall, 1973.

A combination of crazy riddles with unexpected answers and funny rhymes with silly exaggerated illustrations. "What's purple, weighs two tons, and lives at the bottom of the sea? Moby Grape." "How can you prevent an elephant from charging? Take away his charge card."

Had enough? One more to really whet your appetite. "If an athlete gets athlete's foot, what does an astronaut get? Missile toe."

DAFFYNITIONS by Charles Keller (editor). Illus. by F. A. Fitzgerald. Englewood Cliffs, N. J.: Prentice-Hall 1976.

Crazy definitions with cartoon illustrations using familiar words
afford—a car some people drive
denial—where Cleopatra lived
snoring—sheet music

MIND YOUR OWN BUSINESS by Michael Rosen. Illus. by Quentin Blake. Charham, N.Y.: S. G. Phillips, 1974.

Wonderful childhood adventure poetry told by the boy narrator with Blake's usual hilarious illustrations. It is a wonder how he turns black and white strokes into children with shaggy hair, baggy pants and seemingly all arms and legs.

THE BIRTHDAY COW by Eve Meriam. Illus. by Guy Michel. New York: Alfred A. Knopf, 1978.

Light, funny poems about familiar things that illustrate why Meriam's poetry is so appealing to children.

A BOOK OF NONSENSE by Edward Lear. Illus. by Brian Holme. New York: Viking, 1980.

The master and the originator of the limerick after more than a hundred years is still delighting young and old alike. Lear's verses are still the funniest and the best and the drawings suit them admirably. (Several paperbacks available.)

LAUGHABLE LIMERICKS by Sarah and John E. Brewton (editors). Illus. by Ingrid Fetz. New York: Thomas Y. Crowell Company, 1965.

More limericks designed to introduce children to the joys of humorous poetry. Old people, young people, and animals all combine in an illogical, impossible, hilarious collection of the oldest form of funny verse.

MY TANG'S TUNGLED AND OTHER RIDICULOUS SITUATIONS by Sarah and John Brewton and G. Meredith Blackburn III (editors). Illus. by Graham Booth. New York: Harper and Row, 1973.

A collection of humorous poems ranging from tongue twisters and limericks to narrative poems and rhyming poems. Includes works by Lewis Carroll, Ogden Nash, T. S. Eliot, and A. A. Milne. Selections range from the ridiculous to the absurd and defy the mind and the tongue. "I often pause and wonder, At fate's peculiar ways, For nearly all our famous men, Were born on holidays" (Anon.).

A TWISTER OF TWISTS, A TANGLER OF TONGUES by Alvin Schwartz. New York: Lippincott Jr. Books, 1972.

Short and long tongue twisters designed to delight children who love to play with words. "Selfish shellfish." "The sixth sheik's sixth sheep's sick."

PIGERICKS by Arnold Lobel. New York: Harper and Row, 1983.

Lobel uses the form made famous by Lear to create a zany collection of limericks, using pigs as the main characters. The meshing of brightly colored illustrations and witty rhymes will delight young poetry readers. The mustachioed and spectacled pig with a pen looks suspiciously like the author/illustrator.

LOONY LIMERICKS by Jack Stokes. Garden City, N.Y.: Doubleday, 1978.
An American twist to an old form. Puns and gags in limerick form but not the usual Lear-type nonsense. Fun!

THE MEAN OLD MEAN HYENA by Jack Prelutsky. Illus. by Arnold Lobel. New York: Greenwillow, 1978.
Plays on words, repetitions, rhymes, and evil combine to make mischievous fun. The mean hyena plays dirty tricks on some animals until the elephant catches him in his trunk and he plays the dirtiest trick of all.

NIGHTMARES: POEMS TO TROUBLE YOUR SLEEP by Jack Prelutsky. Illus. by Arnold Lobel. New York: Greenwillow, 1976.
Scary poems using rolling, picturesque language coupled with black and white illustrations bound to make a child scream with delight. Prelutsky and Lobel are a great team. Freud would love it!

THE HAIRY BOOK by Babette Cole. New York: Methuen Children's Books, 1987.
Hairy everything from bogs and frogs and coats and goats to hairy nice and hairy scary. Rhyming romp through a hairy world seen through the eyes of a hairless lad.

THE LAUGH BOOK by Joanna Cole and Stephanie Calmenson (editors). Illus. by Marylin Hafner. Garden City, N.Y.: Doubleday, 1986.
A collection of jokes, riddles, knock knocks, puzzles, and games that add up to a treasury of laugh makers. Some of the best are found between the covers, including Shel Silverstein, Lewis Carroll, Edward Lear, and Ogden Nash. This is really an unusual collection since it includes

actual excerpts from some of the funniest books for children. Included are Judy Blume, Beverly Cleary, Judith Viorst, and Charles Schultz among others. The wonderful illustrations are all black and white and mesh happily with the text. A worthwhile investment for every family.

ROBERT MUNSCH

From Canada we welcome author Robert Munsch and his delightful stories for young children. Pleasing to the eye as well as to the funnybone, they depict the trials of little ones when faced with ordinary day-by-day events.

THOMAS' SNOWSUIT by Robert Munsch. Illus. by Michael Martchenko. Ontario, Canada: Annick Press (distributed by Firefly Books Ltd.), 1985.

Just a peek at Thomas's determined face lets you know who will win the battle in this story. Thomas hates his new snowsuit and has made up his mind not to wear it. When his teacher tries to get Thomas to wear it out to recess, an enormous fight ensues. When it is finally over, Thomas is wearing the teacher's dress and the teacher is wearing—you guessed it—Thomas's snowsuit! The battle resumes with a new entrant in the fray—the principal. You can just imagine the result. Children will love the way Thomas handles a very common problem.

50 BELOW ZERO by Robert Munsch. Illus. by Michael Martchenko. Ontario, Canada: Annick Press (distributed by Firefly Books, Ltd.), 1986.

Jason's father walks in his sleep with dangerous results. Jason finds him on top of the refrigerator, in the garage on top of the car, and leaning against a tree in the snow. In typical small-boy fashion, Jason finds a simple solution that allows him to keep tabs on his father. The surprise ending shows how like his father Jason really is. Children will love feeling superior to Dad and watching Jason take charge of the situation.

MUD PUDDLE by Robert Munsch. Illus. by Sami Suomalainen. Ontario, Canada: Annick Press (distributed by Firefly Books, Ltd.), 1982.

Little Julie Ann has a problem. A sneaky mud puddle keeps slipping up behind her and covering her from head to toe with mud. Mommy keeps cleaning her up and that nasty old mud puddle finds her each time. But Julie Ann finally outsmarts the wily puddle with a well-placed bar of soap. Delicious little fantasy with its roots in realism. Wouldn't every child like to tangle with a mud puddle?

THE PAPER BAG PRINCESS by Robert Munsch. Illus. by Michael Martchenko. Ontario, Canada: Annick Press (distributed by Firefly Books, Ltd.), 1980.

Wonderful fantasy about Princess Elizabeth and Prince Ronald. Familar names? Unfortunately, an evil dragon burns all of the princess's clothes and carries Prince Ronald away. Elizabeth vows to get Ronald back and puts on the only thing in the castle that was not burned—a paper bag. After a series of comical confrontations, Elizabeth tires the dragon out so completely that she is able to enter his cave and free Prince Ronald. But instead of being overjoyed, Ronald scolds Elizabeth for her unsuitable dress and her messy hair. They do not live happily ever after. Terrific parody of typical prince-and-princess stories.

Also from Canada, a collection reminiscent of Roald Dahl.

SCARY POEMS FOR ROTTEN KIDS by Sean O'Huigin. Windsor: Black Moss Press, 1987.

Monsters, skeletons, and snakes slither across the pages of this deliciously frightening book of poems. Children will love this comical collection of verse designed for giggles rather than tears. Delightful cartoon-style illustrations.